THEN & NOW

LAGUNA BEACH

Opposite: This c. 1897 image shows the beginnings of the town of Laguna Beach with scattered tents along with some wooden homes on the bluffs, including the first Laguna Beach Hotel. Built in 1895, it is seen just above the beach at right center. The foreground beach area shows the signs of drainage from the Laguna Canyon, which today is channeled underneath Broadway Avenue, opening under the boardwalk. (Image courtesy of the Laguna Beach Historical Society.)

THEN & NOW

LAGUNA BEACH

Foster J. Eubank and Gene Felder

This book is dedicated to Gene's wife, Johanna, for her support and encouragement and to their grandchildren, Annalyse, Landon, Alexander, Caylani, and Trevor, who all have much history to make.

This book is dedicated to Foster's wife, Harvest, for her support and also to Foster's parents, Ray and Harriett Eubank, for moving their young family to Laguna Beach and allowing Foster to absorb a life that only Laguna Beach can give.

Copyright © 2013 by Foster J. Eubank and Gene Felder
ISBN 978-0-7385-9960-1

Library of Congress Control Number: 2012951692

Published by Arcadia Publishing
Charleston, South Carolina

Printed in the United States of America

Then and Now is a registered trademark and is used under license from Salamander Books Limited

For all general information, please contact Arcadia Publishing:
Telephone 843-853-2070
Fax 843-853-0044
E-mail sales@arcadiapublishing.com
For customer service and orders:
Toll-Free 1-888-313-2665

Visit us on the Internet at www.arcadiapublishing.com

ON THE FRONT COVER: Main Beach has always been popular in Laguna Beach. As early as 1880, Laguna Beach became a popular summer camp, especially for people from Riverside and Santa Ana, who might stay the entire summer. Later, boardinghouses and summer cottages were built, leading to permanent residences. Starting in 1900, noted artists came and stayed, painting Laguna impressionist plein air works and making Laguna Beach known as an art colony. (Then image courtesy of the Laguna Beach Historical Society; now image by Foster Eubank.)

ON THE BACK COVER: Laguna Beach's beautiful coastline of sandy beaches, rocky coves, and tide pools has been an appealing place for visitors to explore. The two children seen in this early photograph were doing just that. Now the Laguna Beach coast is a marine reserve; the guidelines are to touch nothing and leave only footprints. TideWater docents volunteer their time to educate the beach-going public about the life and natural processes occurring in the tidal habitats. (Image courtesy of the Laguna Beach Historical Society.)

Contents

Acknowledgments		vii
Introduction		ix
1.	Laguna's Beach Discovered	11
2.	Laguna Beach Grows and Attracts Famous Artists	21
3.	North Laguna Beach Develops with the New Coast Highway	61
4.	South Laguna Beach Expands Along Its Picturesque Shoreline	77

Acknowledgments

A book of this nature would not be possible without a varied assortment of historic photographs, and many of the ones used in this book came from the photograph archives of the Laguna Beach Historical Society. Use of the society's photograph archive, as well as obtaining accurate historical background for each image used, would not have been possible without the help of coauthor Gene Felder. All "Now" images come from the private collection of coauthor Foster Eubank. Additionally, numerous images came from the Orange County Archives, with Chris Jepsen being instrumental in supplying numerous images, a great many of which came from the Tom Pulley postcard collection. Other images were provided by the Ornage County Public Library and the USC Libraries Digital Lab.

Our window to the past of Laguna Beach is enhanced by the foresight of people like Marilyn Ghere, Merle Ramsey, Anne Frank, Betty Kelly, Jane Norgren, Ken Lauher, Dr. Michael Onorato, Art Sherman, and Rita Wills Thompson. A word of thanks to Bob Blankman, who with the First American Financial Corporation Historical Collection collected, preserved, and generously provided many one-of-a-kind historic images.

Our thanks to James Nordstrom of Silver Images in Laguna Beach for providing many vintage images as well as identification of the historical locations of some of them.

Historic information comes from the city's Historic Resource Inventory and from books written by Joseph S. Thurston, Merle and Mabel Ramsey, and Roger W. Jones, as well as the Cal State Fullerton oral history of Beryl Wilson Viebeck and articles written by Belinda Blacketer and Karen Wilson Turnbull. We are thankful for the assistance of board members of the Laguna Beach Historical Society, including Anne Frank, Eric Jessen, Dr. Glenna Matthews, and Ronald Kaufman. Additional information was provided by former Laguna Beach mayor Ann Christoph. Whenever we had a question concerning the history of an image, Laguna Beach Historical Society board member Jane Petty Janz was the person we contacted. Her knowledge of the historical detail of Laguna's background has been instrumental in correctly identifying the background and location of many photographs used in the book.

We are indebted to Robin D. Williams of R.W. Films in Laguna Beach for spending time with Foster hiking around Laguna Beach and pointing out the locations of various sites used to make historical images. Robin possesses intimate knowledge of the Laguna environs gleaned from a lifetime of walking the entire length and breadth of Laguna. Robin conveyed to us historical information not obtainable elsewhere. Our thanks to lifelong Laguna resident Tom Pletts for allowing us to use his private, and memorable, image of Foster's class of 1954 in front of the Laguna South Coast Theater in 1948. We are grateful to Barbara Nash and her Laguna Beach friends for their generous support in putting this book together.

Lastly, our appreciation to the staff of the historic landmark Hotel Laguna for allowing access to their rooftop to record images of downtown Laguna Beach, some of which are used in this book.

Introduction

Laguna Beach was bordered by the Irvine Ranch to the north and the Rawson (later Moulton) Ranch to the east when homesteaders arrived to claim "government land," which ran south of Laguna Creek down to Three Arch Bay. The ranches were former Mexican land grants Rancho San Joaquin and Rancho Niguel. The first homesteader in South Laguna was Eugene Salter in 1870; he abandoned his claim, which was then proved up by George W. Thurston Sr. Later, the first homesteader in Laguna Beach proper was William Brooks, shortly joined by his brother Lorenzo Nathan (Nate) Brooks. North Laguna, north of Broadway Avenue, was part of the Irvine Ranch but was sold by James Irvine, with Laguna Cliffs developed in 1906 by Howard G. Heisler, L.C. McKnight, and the Thumb brothers.

Today, driving into the city limits of Laguna Beach, signs reading "Laguna Beach Home of the Festival of Arts and Pageant of the Masters" welcome visitors. The first artist visiting Laguna Beach was Norman St. Clair, a noted watercolorist who painted in Laguna Beach in 1900 and had a one-man show in the Laguna Beach Hotel in 1906. More artists came to paint outdoors, or plein air, and Laguna Beach became known as an art colony particularly noted for Laguna impressionism. Led by Edgar Payne and Anna Hills, the Laguna Beach Art Association was founded in 1918. The performing arts were active as well, with the Laguna Playhouse being formed in 1920. Today it is the Laguna Moulton Theatre.

Today, Laguna Beach is home to numerous artists and art galleries. During the summer, there are three art festivals; in addition to the Festival of the Arts, there is the Sawdust Festival and Art-A-Fair. The Laguna Beach Art Association led to the Laguna Art Museum, the Festival of the Arts, the Pageant of the Masters, and an accredited art college. The pageant is a 90-minute performance in the Irvine Bowl amphitheater of "living picture" re-creations of classical and contemporary artworks with real people posing. The college was known as the Art Institute of Southern California but is now the Laguna College of Art and Design.

Laguna Beach is located in Orange County, which broke away from the much larger Los Angeles County in 1889. Most cities in the county just have a line dividing them; however, Laguna Beach is surrounded by 22,000 acres of open space, primarily natural chaparral landscape. This was possible because of the Irvine and Moulton Ranches and thanks to Jim Dilley and the Laguna Greenbelt organization that he founded in 1968. In addition, Laguna Beach has benefited by efforts to promote the village atmosphere; Village Laguna was founded by Arnold Hano in 1971, and in that year, voters limited building heights to a maximum of 36 feet by an overwhelming vote.

The earliest known photographs taken in the southern California area now known as Laguna Beach are from the late 1880s. When viewing these images, one is getting a peek into the history of the area, and if it were not for those people who diligently saved these images, we would never know how the area once appeared. To further appreciate these images of the past, one should know that the cameras of that day were large, heavy, and expensive units mounted on tripods with the images captured by a time-consuming process using fragile glass plates and a complex chemical reaction. This was not available to the general public, but the evolution of the camera was moving fast, and by the early 1900s, the easy-to-use Kodak Brownie camera, at a cost of $1, was introduced along with inexpensive film. Thank goodness for that, for what followed was the general public recording a wealth of images of a changing America, including the future city of Laguna Beach.

Because of its location next to the Pacific Ocean, coupled with its mountainous beauty, Laguna Beach became a magnet for artists, movie stars, and tourists alike. Movie studios making films in the Laguna environs, the professional photographers carrying their bulky cameras, and the tourists with their easy-to-use cameras all recorded Laguna in images. Many of these images fortunately ended up in numerous archives, including the Laguna Beach Historical Society, or in the hands of private citizens. Only through those early-day images can we see and appreciate Laguna's growth and its historic past.

This book presents vintage photographs of Laguna's early days alongside modern-day images taken at the same locations. Much has changed; however, much has been preserved.

Chapter 1

Laguna's Beach Discovered

Laguna Beach was a seven-mile stretch of government land available for homesteading. Large ranches from Mexican land grants were to both the north (Rancho San Joaquin, later Irvine Ranch) and east (Rancho Niguel, later Moulton Ranch). Homesteaders came beginning in 1870, and the area became three towns with three post offices. The first postmasters were William Brooks in Laguna Beach (1891), Oliver Brooks in Arch Beach (1889), and postmistress Grace Powers in South Laguna (1933). George Rogers homesteaded (1880) and subdivided (1887) the downtown area, which includes most of Main Beach shown in this c. 1910 photograph.

By the late 1800s and early 1900s, when this photograph was taken, Laguna's Main Beach was a popular camping spot for the folks who lived in inland communities like Riverside. Some camped out on the beach for the entire summer and could fish or pick abalone off the rocks. Today, camping is not allowed on Laguna's beaches, and the coastal marine environment is a preserve to "protect, maintain, enhance, and restore California's marine ecosystems for their ecological values and their use and enjoyment by the public."

LAGUNA'S BEACH DISCOVERED

This 1920s image shows the north side of downtown Laguna Beach with part of the Main Beach at the right and the undeveloped hills in the background. Car parking and camping on the beach was common. The left building was the Pomona College Marine Laboratory, built in 1913, and the dark building on the far right was the Sayles dance hall. Today, the original Pomona Laboratory site is a gas station, and part of what was the Main Beach is now covered by the basketball courts.

Laguna's Beach Discovered

Early in the development of Laguna Beach, homes were allowed on the beach with the proper set-back. This 1910s Main Beach photograph shows a series of homes, with homesteader Lorenzo Nathan (Nate) Brooks's house at the left. Nate Brooks came to Laguna Beach in 1876, married Catherine Skidmore in 1899, and moved his house to this location on a lot purchased for $50 from George Rogers. At right is the Joseph Yoch Laguna Beach Hotel, which today is the Hotel Laguna.

When this photograph was taken in 1910, the children of noted early Santa Ana attorney E.E. Keech were enjoying a day at Main Beach. The view, taken from the Bird Rock area, shows Laguna's Main Beach in the background. Then as now, families with their children have great fun walking on rock outcroppings and exploring the sea life found in tide pools. Today, rules are in place to protect the tide pool life, making sure future generations will enjoy the same experience as people did in 1910.

Laguna's Beach Discovered

The old wooden Yoch Laguna Beach Hotel, seen in this early 1900s view, was built in 1895 on the southern part of Laguna's Main Beach. The hotel in the early days was more than just a place to sleep. Steak broils, teas, moonlight rides, and even horseback riding to the local mountains were all common offerings. The present Hotel Laguna, located at 425 South Coast Highway at Laguna Avenue, was built in 1930 and is still a vital economic force in the growth of Laguna Beach.

Ladies of leisure are seen enjoying tennis in this early 1900s photograph near the Yoch Laguna Beach Hotel, seen in the background. While recreation and entertainment were limited in the early days, the hotel itself had a small additional building (a pavilion and later an art gallery) that served as the unofficial city hall and for weddings, dances, funerals, and the meeting place for religious services. Today, the old tennis court is now El Paseo Street, with the Main Beach Park tot lot playground on the right. The Hotel Laguna, built in 1930, is in the background.

About 1895, Joseph and Catherine Yoch brought two hotels from other sites to this location, now 425 South Coast Highway, and built them together in the form seen in this early 1900s photograph. The Yoch Laguna Beach Hotel drew notables despite the fact that it had 30 bedrooms and only two bathrooms. In 1930, the old hotel was replaced by the current Hotel Laguna, which was built in the Mission Revival style. Architecturally and historically, this is Laguna's single most outstanding landmark building.

This c. 1930s photograph was taken from an upper floor of Hotel Laguna looking northwest with a view of Laguna's Main Beach. The foreground Café Las Ondas was designed by architect Aubrey St. Clair and built in 1927. This building, along with numerous other buildings designed by St. Clair, was said to have "set the tone and style for much of what we consider to be the best qualities of Laguna Beach's village character," according to former Laguna Beach mayor Ann Christoph. Today, the site is part of the city's "Window to the Sea," Main Beach Park.

Beach play and bathing suit style on Laguna's Main Beach is displayed in this 1920s photograph. This image shows the existing oceanfront structures, including the old wooden Laguna Beach Hotel, seen towards the left. In the older days, the Main Beach area was privately owned and had dance halls, restaurants, and gas stations. Adults and children alike frolicked on the beach. Today, more structures have been built on the bluff, but the beach itself still looks about the same.

LAGUNA'S BEACH DISCOVERED

CHAPTER 2

LAGUNA BEACH GROWS AND ATTRACTS FAMOUS ARTISTS

This photograph is of Forest Avenue from South Coast Boulevard on July 4, 1920. The first artist who came to Laguna Beach was noted watercolorist Norman St. Clair about 1900. Word spread, and thanks to the leadership of Edgar Payne and Anna Hills, the Laguna Beach Art Association was founded in 1918 and Laguna Beach was recognized as an art colony. Today, there are three summer art festivals, the Festival of the Arts and Pageant of the Masters since 1933, the Laguna Art Museum, and the Laguna College of Art and Design.

This 1918 photograph looks west down Forest Avenue towards the ocean. The building at the right foreground was the Laguna Beach Lumber Company, which was founded in 1912 by Joseph Jahraus. The lumber operations moved to Laguna Canyon in 1975 and were sold to Ganahl in 2001. Today, the Laguna Lumber Company office is the Lumberyard Restaurant. The building at the center by the trees in the old photograph was the Little Brown Laguna Chapel, built in 1915; today, it is the 1928-built Community Presbyterian Church at Second Street.

Laguna Beach Grows and Attracts Famous Artists

The beginnings of downtown Laguna Beach are seen in this c. 1917 photograph taken from St. Mary's Episcopal Church area on Park Avenue looking north. At right center is the Little Brown Laguna Chapel, and the road going from right center to the left is Forest Avenue. To the left of the chapel and lined by trees is Second Street. The Little Brown Laguna Chapel was replaced in 1928 by the Community Presbyterian Church, built at 415 Second Street in the Gothic-inspired Mediterranean Revival architectural style.

LAGUNA BEACH GROWS AND ATTRACTS FAMOUS ARTISTS 23

The old ranch house seen in this early 1900s image was originally built in 1880 and was the home of George Rogers. The pepper tree seen on the left was planted by Rogers and his daughter Lizzie about the same time the home was built. The property was bought in 1927 by the Woman's Club of Laguna Beach and sold to the City of Laguna Beach in 1950. The city hall was built here at 505 Forest Avenue and is pictured with the same historic pepper tree.

Laguna Beach Grows and Attracts Famous Artists

Looking east on a dirt Ocean Avenue in this early 1920s photograph, the United States Tires garage with gas pumps is seen on the right. The hills show no residential development except for a human-planted eucalyptus grove at the top and the "Temple Hills" sign at left center. Today, the avenue is a busy two-way street, and the former garage area is now occupied by Hennessey's Tavern at 213 Ocean Avenue and Areo gifts and home accessories store at 207 Ocean Avenue.

LAGUNA BEACH GROWS AND ATTRACTS FAMOUS ARTISTS

In the 1930s, the corner of Coast Highway and Forest Avenue had become so busy with automobile traffic that an officer standing on a rock was needed to control the traffic. Beryl Wilson Viebect notes that George Rogers and other homesteaders included planting eucalyptus trees as part of their effort to prove up their claim, and the groves gave the street the name Forest Avenue. They mistakenly thought the eucalyptus wood would be good for rail ties and building materials. Today, the hillside is Mystic Hills, which lost about 200 homes during the October 27, 1993, Laguna wildfire.

LAGUNA BEACH GROWS AND ATTRACTS FAMOUS ARTISTS

The corner of Forest Avenue and Park Avenue is one of the most recognizable locations in Laguna Beach. Going back to 1915, this site has undergone several changes from a pharmacy to the present day Chantilly Ice Cream store at 202 Park Avenue. Still there is a hanging gate with a poem that reads: "This gate hangs well and hinders none, refresh and rest, then travel on." From 1915 to 1921, the gate was at other downtown sites; in 1921, D.L. Rankin bought the store and displayed the gate here.

Laguna Beach Grows and Attracts Famous Artists

This 1920s view looking south shows the White House Restaurant on the left, while the Yoch Laguna Beach Hotel is hidden amongst the eucalyptus trees on the right. The White House Restaurant at 340 South Coast Highway was founded in 1918 by Claude Bronner and is the oldest continuously operating restaurant in Laguna Beach. Today, the White House Restaurant is still at the same location, but it is partially obscured in the modern photograph by the small shop at the corner. The Hotel Laguna is at right.

Laguna Beach Grows and Attracts Famous Artists

The Fred Clapp General Store, seen in this c. 1920s photograph, was built in 1915 and located at 225 Forest Avenue. It was written on the photograph that "a customer could purchase anything from wheels for the buggy, meat for the table, material for the latest styles or sit down to a great meal." The Clapp family is among the earliest settlers and important founding families of Laguna Beach. Today, this location is a two-level Nike sportswear store.

LAGUNA BEACH GROWS AND ATTRACTS FAMOUS ARTISTS

This early 1940s photograph looks up North Coast Highway from Forest Avenue and shows Hotel Laguna and a series of shops. The Hotel Laguna's neon sign was a beacon to all but was removed in 1996. In 1985, the hotel was purchased by Claes Andersen, who refurbished the interior and exterior of this "Grand Old Lady" and created an award-winning establishment with a European flair. It was said that during the early days of this hotel, it was used as a hideaway by many dignitaries and movie industry people.

This 1920s photograph shows a two-story building at the left on the corner of Ocean Avenue and South Coast Highway. This building was the real estate office of Clifford "Gavy" Cravath, who was a major-league baseball star and the top National League home run hitter for seven years from 1913 to 1920. Gavy invested in Laguna's real estate and was justice of the peace and active in city affairs, including getting adequate water to the city. Today, the building still stands as the Fiori, featuring Italian ceramics.

Laguna Beach Grows and Attracts Famous Artists

The building at 180 South Coast Highway is directly across from the center of Laguna Beach's Main Beach. In 1950, when this photograph was taken, it was the Carpenter's Day & Night Market and a five-and-dime store full of knickknacks. Today, a small clothing boutique called Tight Assets occupies the former Carpenter's, and a Starbucks resides at the former five-and-dime. To the left and out of the photograph is the Laguna Beach South Coast Cinema.

LAGUNA BEACH GROWS AND ATTRACTS FAMOUS ARTISTS

The 1924 image of the northeast end of Forest Avenue comes from the Merle Ramsey Photograph Collection. The intersection in the image had been noted as Broadway and Forest Avenues by Ramsey, but Broadway Avenue was not built until the 1930s. Regardless, it was the major entrance into the city prior to the State Coast Highway being built in 1926 connecting to Newport Beach. Today, it is the intersection of Ocean and Forest Avenues, with Laguna Canyon Road and the Irvine Bowl Park in the distance.

Laguna Beach Grows and Attracts Famous Artists

The 1950s photograph shows Laguna Tire Company at what is now 480 Ocean Avenue at the corner of Forest Avenue. The owner, Mr. Fisher, stands next to a truck that was used to collect tires from the local garages and bring them back to the business for recapping. Coauthor Foster Eubank worked here for $1 an hour in 1953. The building today is the Forest and Ocean Gallery with an outside sculpture, one of many artworks in public places thanks to the arts commission and the Community Art Project.

Laguna Beach Grows and Attracts Famous Artists

The Laguna Beach High School class of 1954 is seen in this 1948 photograph (Foster Eubank's sixth-grade class) in front of the South Coast Theater at 162 South Coast Highway. The theater was built in 1934 by Fred Aufdenkamp and opened in 1935 with a ceremonial extravaganza attended by a throng of locals and several movie stars. The first movie shown was *Ginger*, starring Jane Withers. Today, the other two Aufdenkamp theaters are gone, but the South Coast Theater still shows first-run movies at the same location.

LAGUNA BEACH GROWS AND ATTRACTS FAMOUS ARTISTS

In 1952, Richard Nixon, a US senator from California, campaigned in Laguna Beach as Dwight Eisenhower's vice presidential running mate. The photograph shows Nixon along with his wife, Patricia (to the right of Nixon) in front of the Laguna Beach City Hall at 505 Forest Avenue.

The pepper tree at left was planted in 1881 by pioneer George Rogers and one of his daughters, Lizzie. Their house in later years was bought by the Woman's Club. In 1951, the city demolished the old ranch house and built the present city hall but preserved the tree.

LAGUNA BEACH GROWS AND ATTRACTS FAMOUS ARTISTS

The 1916 photograph looks east toward the mouth of Laguna Canyon; what is now Broadway Avenue was originally swamp-like and received water from Laguna Creek, which drains Laguna Canyon. Today, the creek is underground and drains into the ocean, and Broadway Avenue has become one of the main traffic arteries from the Laguna Canyon Road into Laguna Beach. The traffic signal is at Beach Street, which due to its history, does not go straight across Broadway Avenue.

Laguna Beach Grows and Attracts Famous Artists

This c. 1926 photograph was recorded looking north at the corner of Forest Avenue and South Coast Highway and clearly shows the ocean side (left) of the highway lined with numerous businesses that blocked the view of the beach. In 1968, the City of Laguna Beach purchased this 1,000-foot-long oceanfront property for $3,135,000, later removing all businesses. The Main Beach Park was dedicated on June 22, 1974. Today, this "Window to the Sea" allows for an unobstructed view of the Pacific Ocean for drivers and pedestrians alike.

Laguna Beach Grows and Attracts Famous Artists

A 1953 parade down Broadway Avenue was a project to raise money to install lights on the high school football field. The float featured football player Ronald Adel and cheerleaders Carole Davis (kneeling), Mimi Moorhead (upper left), and Carol Van Buren (upper center). Posing at the far right is Stanley Allen, owner of the Allen Motor Company, seen in the right background. At the left background is the Sprouse-Reitz store at 229 Broadway Avenue, which today is the Union Bank; Allen Motors, at 217 Broadway Avenue, is now the Food Village.

LAGUNA BEACH GROWS AND ATTRACTS FAMOUS ARTISTS

This c. 1929 photograph taken from the tower of Hotel Laguna looking north shows the heart of downtown Laguna Beach. The Sandwich Mill restaurant, seen at the lower center, occupied the prime corner of South Coast Highway and Forest Avenue. This valuable site was owned by Ora and Oscar Warling, and the restaurant attracted travelers, movie stars of the day, and locals alike. Eventually, the Warlings leased this site to the Bank of America, and today, it houses the Fingerhut Gallery.

Laguna Beach Grows and Attracts Famous Artists

This house at 289 Laguna Avenue at the corner of Glenneyre Street, built in 1905, was the home of Nick and Kathryne Isch, who were grandparents of Laguna Beach Historical Society board member Jane Petty Janz. Isch first came to California in 1888 to visit his sister, Catherine Yoch. In 1895, he opened the general store and post office at the other end of this block, now site of the Heisler Building. The post office was designated "Lagona," and it was Isch who effected the name change to Laguna Beach in 1904.

Laguna Beach Grows and Attracts Famous Artists

It's hard to believe there are more cars in the c. 1920s photograph than the modern one. This is Laguna Avenue looking east across South Coast Highway to Park Avenue. The historic photograph certainly was taken prior to 1930, since the Heisler Building is not yet built. This site was very busy and included Nick Isch's grocery store, then the Mills Café, and the Villa prior to the Heisler Building being constructed in 1931. The eucalyptus trees at the far right were removed when the Hotel Laguna was built in 1930.

Laguna Beach Grows and Attracts Famous Artists

The Heisler Building's original owner was Howard G. Heisler. It was built in 1931 across the street from the Hotel Laguna. Built in the Provincial Revival style with steep-pitched gables and a modified turret on the corner, this building contributed greatly to the village quality of downtown Laguna Beach. Beginning in 1935, Rawson's Drug Store occupied the corner portion at 400 South Coast Highway (seen in the early 1940s photograph); it was later changed to the Jolly Roger restaurant. Today, the Tommy Bahama restaurant is in the renovated building.

LAGUNA BEACH GROWS AND ATTRACTS FAMOUS ARTISTS

43

In 1912, 23-year-old Joseph R. Jahraus opened the Laguna Lumber Company (the oldest continuous business in the city) at the bend of Forest Avenue to supply wood for the growing city. In 1919, Joe and his father, Elmer (a cigar maker and real estate agent who handled the sale of Emerald Bay), built the beautiful French Normandy building seen in the 1930 photograph. Today, this same historic building is located at 384 Forest Avenue and is the popular Lumberyard Restaurant, with the Lumberyard Mall at the west end.

Laguna Beach Grows and Attracts Famous Artists

The Laguna Playhouse was built in 1924 at 319 Ocean Avenue. During World War II, it was used to entertain troops, and throughout the 1950s and 1960s, staged productions featuring many movie stars of the day were presented. In 1969, the building was demolished, and the Moulton Theatre was built at 606 Laguna Canyon Road near the Festival of Arts. Today, the parking lot retains a pepper tree and the original theater's callboard. The Community Presbyterian Church, built in 1928, is at the right in both photographs.

Laguna Beach Grows and Attracts Famous Artists

Through the 1950s, most of Ocean Avenue in downtown Laguna Beach was residential. The home seen in the 1925 photograph at 278 Ocean Avenue (built in 1923) is one of the few old beach houses remaining in the downtown proper. The original owner, Vernon Murphy, is seen in the photograph along with Gladys Blacketer Paine at left and Floy Blacketer Gilbert at right. In 1935, Blanch Clapp Smith's mother bought the home. Today, the renovated Murphy-Smith House is home to the Laguna Beach Historical Society and open to the public.

The lifeguard tower found today on the Main Beach is the most recognizable of many landmark buildings found in Laguna Beach and is locally significant to historic preservationists. The 1930s photograph shows a gas station office at the original location of the tower at the corner of Coast Highway and Broadway Avenue. The lifeguards acquired the building from the abandoned gas station during the Depression and moved it in 1937 across the street to Main Beach. Over the years, it has undergone several alterations.

LAGUNA BEACH GROWS AND ATTRACTS FAMOUS ARTISTS

"A Towering Icon, the historic Main Beach Tower stands as the symbol for Laguna Beach," according to the *Laguna Beach Magazine*. The 1953 image shows the tower on what was then the Main Beach boardwalk serving as a lifeguard station, as it still does today. The boardwalk had numerous concessions over the years, and at the time this photograph was taken, there was the Beachcomber Gift Shop in the Hotel de la Costa at 185 Boardwalk, and to its left was a bowling alley built in the previous Cabrillo Ballroom Dance Hall.

Laguna Beach Grows and Attracts Famous Artists

The United States was just climbing out of a recession when Pres. Franklin D. Roosevelt's motorcade came through Laguna Beach on July 14, 1938. The president was directly in front of what was then the White House Café on Coast Highway, and shortly thereafter, when the motorcade stopped, he was presented a Laguna impressionist seascape by local artist Frank Cuprien. Today, the renovated White House Café still stands along with a gift shop extension at 300 South Coast Highway called Things and Carats.

Laguna Beach Grows and Attracts Famous Artists

The historic photograph is from 1939 or later and shows, in the foreground, the Laguna Beach High School at 625 Park Avenue, constructed in 1935. The elementary school was built at this site in 1928, with high school students bused to Tustin. The historic photograph also shows the newer elementary school across the street on the north side of Park Avenue; the building now houses district offices. The Laguna Beach Unified School District consists of the high school, one middle school, and two elementary schools.

 LAGUNA BEACH GROWS AND ATTRACTS FAMOUS ARTISTS

The Laguna Beach Fire Station, seen in this late 1930s photograph, was built in 1931 at 501 Forest Avenue. The firemen standing out front were part of an all-volunteer department created in 1919 by Laguna's first fire chief, Anthony Derkum. The fire truck seen at left was a Seagrave with a 500-gallon-per-minute pump. Today, the City of Laguna Beach Fire Department employs at staff of 41 full-time personnel, and the fire truck garage doors are now rectangular to accommodate bigger modern fire engines.

LAGUNA BEACH GROWS AND ATTRACTS FAMOUS ARTISTS

One of the first post offices to be used in Laguna Beach was in the Isch store, on the site of the Heisler Building (now home of the Tommy Bahama restaurant) on the southeast corner of Laguna Avenue and South Coast Highway. Later, several other locations in Laguna Beach were used as post offices; one, built in 1938, is seen in this photograph at 298 Broadway Avenue. This post office was closed within a few years because of traffic problems. Commercial uses followed, and today, the building is Buck's Fine Art.

The modern photograph shows St. Mary's Episcopal Church at 428 Park Avenue. Next door at 430 Park Avenue is St. Francis by the Sea American Catholic Cathedral. The 1930s photograph shows the original church, built by Percy Wise Clarkson in 1925 and demolished in 1979. Clarkson left that congregation and in 1933 built St. Francis by the Sea American Catholic Cathedral. Today it is one of two American Catholic cathedrals in the country and a well-known historical landmark visited by tourists from all over the world.

LAGUNA BEACH GROWS AND ATTRACTS FAMOUS ARTISTS

This early 1920s image shows Edna Kleitsch at the Kleitsch Academy at what is today the corner of Through and Legion Streets. The building was at one time the old Mormon schoolhouse, originally located at Laguna Canyon Road and El Toro Road before being moved three times. Edna's husband, Joseph, was a renowned artist, and together they moved to California in 1920 and settled in Laguna Beach, establishing the Kleitsch Academy, where they both taught and were active in the Laguna art community. Today, this location is the Little Church by the Sea.

A two-room schoolhouse was built in 1908 on the south side of Park Avenue, but in 1928, to make way for a newly built grammar school, the old two-room schoolhouse was moved to 384 Legion Street, where it became Legion Hall. In 1935, Laguna Beach High School became part of the existing Laguna Elementary School facility, and the portion of the school from kindergarten to fifth grade was relocated to a new elementary school built across Park Avenue, seen in the c. 1939 photograph, that is now district offices and a municipal pool.

LAGUNA BEACH GROWS AND ATTRACTS FAMOUS ARTISTS 55

Around 1878, Harvey Hemenway and his family homesteaded 500 acres in the area off of Laguna Canyon Road, building a two-story home on the corner of what is now Arroyo Road and Canyon Acres Drive. The house was later owned by "Old Dad" Fisher, who covered the original house with eucalyptus logs. Later, Anita Skidmore McElree lived there from 1916 to 1920. The historic home, seen in the late 1940s, was torn down in the late 1960s and today nothing remains.

Laguna Beach Grows and Attracts Famous Artists

The Ladd home, seen in this 1890s image, is on Laguna Canyon Road near El Toro Road (to the left, out of picture). It was part of the Mormon settlement led in 1876 by homesteader Andrew Wesley Thompson (1844–1939), a Mormon preacher and Civil War veteran. A water source nearby allowed for farming, but economic boom and bust caused them to move away in 1892, taking their homes with them. Today, Anneliese's School occupies most of the area at 20062 Laguna Canyon Road (right foreground).

Laguna Beach Grows and Attracts Famous Artists

In 1960, the Laguna Beach School of Art and Design, seen at the top of the crosswalk, was located at 606 Laguna Canyon Road. To the right of the school is the City of Laguna Beach's Irvine Bowl Park, which serves as the Festival of the Arts grounds with the Pageant of the Masters shown each summer. The Art Institute of Southern California, now Laguna College of Art and Design, was moved farther out on the Laguna Canyon Road, and today, in its place, is the Laguna Playhouse Moulton Theater.

The 1960s image shows the Irvine Bowl, home of the Festival of Arts and Pageant of the Masters. The Pageant of the Masters, conceived by artist Lolita Perine in 1933 and perfected by artist-builder Roy Ropp beginning in 1935, was held at various makeshift venues within the city. It finally settled at the present site in 1941 on land donated by James Irvine. It was resumed in 1946, following World War II, and every year until the present day it has been presented from after Independence Day until before Labor Day.

Laguna Beach Grows and Attracts Famous Artists

In this early 1920s photograph, there was no Coast Highway in Laguna Beach. There was the Van Syckle Hawaiian arts-and-crafts-style home (built in 1917) at the center of the image; this is now the Cottage Restaurant at the corner of Aster Street and North Coast Highway. In 1926, a one-lane oiled Coast Highway connecting Newport Beach with Laguna Beach was built, and it was paved in 1932 with two lanes in each direction. The house was called San Souci ("without stress") when lived in by Joe Skidmore.

LAGUNA BEACH GROWS AND ATTRACTS FAMOUS ARTISTS

CHAPTER 3

North Laguna Beach Develops with the New Coast Highway

North of Laguna Creek was the 100,000-acre Irvine Ranch. In 1905, Howard G. Heisler and partners purchased North Laguna from James Irvine and promoted the Laguna Cliffs development, the only one with water to each lot. North Laguna even has a castle, now at 770 Hillcrest Drive. Pyne Castle, originally the 62-room Broadview Villa, was built for Walter Estel Pyne, who made money selling player pianos and who struck oil near Yorba Linda. Construction began in 1927 and took seven years. It was converted into the Pyne Castle Apartments in the 1960s. It was restored by Roland Greene and Richard Massen.

Automobile traffic on Coast Highway in 1927 seemed no different than today's traffic. The historic view looks south down Coast Highway showing the Main Beach area where, according to Laguna Beach Historical Society president emerita Belinda Blacketer, the Cabrillo Ballroom Dance Hall was built in 1926. This beach area also had, at different times, auto dealerships, gas stations, hotels, and restaurants. The beachfront was purchased by the city in 1968 and is now the "Window to the Sea," allowing for an unobstructed view of the Pacific.

North Laguna Beach Develops with the New Coast Highway

The Woman's Club of Laguna Beach is seen in this 1924 photograph having a picnic on a bluff just north of downtown Laguna Beach near Heisler Point. Victor Hugo Inn opened on this site in 1938 and is now the popular Las Brisas Restaurant. The Woman's Club was founded in 1922 and played an important role in the early development of Laguna Beach. Its clubhouse was where city hall now stands. The Woman's Club is still active in community affairs, with its clubhouse located on St. Ann's Drive.

NORTH LAGUNA BEACH DEVELOPS WITH THE NEW COAST HIGHWAY

The Laguna Art Museum, located at 307 Cliff Drive, was an outgrowth of the Laguna Beach Art Association, founded in 1918 and spearheaded by artist Edgar Payne. Through Payne's interest in Laguna and its artists, the town became a popular art colony in the 1920s and 1930s. However, it was artist Anna Hill's leadership that was responsible for the art gallery being built in 1928. Since that time, the museum, seen in the early 1940s photograph, has undergone several renovations to reach its modern-day appearance.

The building at the northwest corner of Aster and North Coast Highway was constructed in 1917 by the Van Syckles family. They had vacationed in Hawaii and then had the home constructed. It is considered a landmark building characterized by its sweeping oriental rooflines. The architecture is Japo-Swiss Traditional. This home later served as the residence for the pioneer developer and civic leader Joe Skidmore. In 1938, the building became the Laguna Vista Café, and in 1957, it became the Pancake Cottage. By 1964, it was changed to the Cottage Restaurant, which has recently closed.

The staff of Victor Hugo Inn, along with owners Marcel Langlois and his wife, Pauline, seen at the far left, gathered on the ocean side of the inn for this 1950s photograph. This photograph is courtesy of Betty Kelly, whose mother worked as a waitress at the inn. The original image shows some of the building features such as the large circular wings faced with windowpanes to maximize the panoramic ocean vista. Today's renovated Las Brisas has improved the ocean-view windows.

Beginning in 1887, four piers were built in Laguna Beach within a span of 83 years, and two of those were at Main Beach from Heisler Point to Bird Rock. The first Main Beach Pier was constructed in 1896 and extended to the rocks approximately 500 feet offshore. This pier was replaced by a larger pier designed by Tony Derkum in 1926 that measured 1,150 feet. In 1939, a severe winter storm badly damaged the pier, and it had to be demolished. Despite eight miles of coastline, Laguna today has no pier.

NORTH LAGUNA BEACH DEVELOPS WITH THE NEW COAST HIGHWAY

Great views are available from the gazebo at Heisler Point, named after Howard G. Heisler, who in 1905 purchased North Laguna from the Irvine Company and developed it as the Laguna Cliffs subdivision in 1906 along with partners L.C. McKnight and the Thumb brothers. Lots along the top of the coastal bluff covering approximately 18.5 acres became Heisler Park, which includes planted areas, meandering paths, viewpoints, gazebos, and access to the ocean. Howard G. Heisler served on city council from 1934 to 1939, serving as mayor in 1938.

North Laguna Beach Develops with the New Coast Highway

The c. 1910 photograph shows women and girls standing on an earthen extension from a bluff with Bird Rock behind them. Where they are standing is now part of Heisler Park, named after Howard G. Heisler. At some point Heisler had second thoughts, and a lawsuit by Elmer Jahraus made the park a reality. The actual spot where the women and girls were standing is gone.

NORTH LAGUNA BEACH DEVELOPS WITH THE NEW COAST HIGHWAY

When California road-building bond acts were passed in the 1920s, the Pacific Coast Highway was extended southward from Los Angeles. In 1924, the Irvine Company deeded the right-of-way of its old coast road from Corona del Mar to Laguna Beach to the California Highway Department.

This photograph shows part of the dedication ceremonies of the Coast Highway on October 9, 1926, near Boat Canyon. Movie stars Mary Pickford and Douglas Fairbanks tied together two ribbons, uniting the beach communities of Corona del Mar and Laguna Beach.

70   NORTH LAGUNA BEACH DEVELOPS WITH THE NEW COAST HIGHWAY

The hut seen in this early 1920s photograph was built by two fishermen, Refugio Coronado and Jovancio Duarte, around 1913. Cowboy movie star Tom Mix's house is on the bluff. Today known as Boat Canyon Beach or Fisherman's Cove, it is easily accessible via a stairway next to Diver's Cove at the north end of Heisler Park. For a very small beach, Boat Canyon is seldom crowded during weekdays and is a favorite location for divers and kayakers, but during high tides and big surf, it can be washed out.

NORTH LAGUNA BEACH DEVELOPS WITH THE NEW COAST HIGHWAY

Diver's Cove, found at the north end of Heisler Park, has been popular with beachgoers from the early days of Laguna, when the early 1920s photograph was taken, to the present day. On calm days when the water is clear, snorkeling and scuba diving are popular, as is jumping and diving into the water from the easily accessed rock formation seen in the foreground of today's image.

This early 1930s photograph was taken after road-building bond acts were passed in the 1920s. What followed was the single-lane road seen in this photograph, which was taken just north of Laguna Beach and Emerald Bay. In 1927, Robert Windolph established Tyron's Camp on the beach at El Morro Cove, seen in the photograph.

North Laguna Beach Develops with the New Coast Highway

73

The late 1930s photograph shows the North Coast Highway, built in 1926 (and expanded to two paved lanes in each direction in 1932), at a curve where today's gated community of Emerald Bay is located. The modern image shows part of Emerald Bay, which is unincorporated county land and not part of the city of Laguna Beach. Originally part of the Irvine Ranch, according to a column by Elizabeth H. Quilter (also known as susi Q), the 148.6 acres then called Green Bay was sold to William Miles Sr. and Harry Callender in 1906 for $26,000.

Crescent Bay Beach is found north of Shaw's Cove and south of Emerald Bay in North Laguna Beach. At the north end of this beach is an imposing, steep, rocky cliff, and just offshore is a prominent rock formation called Seal Rock, which is seen in the early 1940s photograph. Crescent Bay and Seal Rock are popular with scuba divers and kayakers, and the modern photograph also shows how avid beachgoers take advantage of this beautiful location.

North Laguna Beach Develops with the New Coast Highway

Laguna's shoreline from what is known today as Sleepy Hollow looking north toward the Main Beach area is nicely displayed in this 1910 photograph. The old Yoch hotel, which today is the rebuilt Hotel Laguna, is seen low on the bluff at center right, and the large building above it to the right has been preserved and was moved in the early 1970s to a lot close to the intersection of Catalina and Cleo Streets.

NORTH LAGUNA BEACH DEVELOPS WITH THE NEW COAST HIGHWAY

CHAPTER 4

SOUTH LAGUNA BEACH EXPANDS ALONG ITS PICTURESQUE SHORELINE

The separate town of Arch Beach around Diamond Street was less than two miles south of downtown Laguna, but wagons could not traverse Bluebird Canyon. This 1916 photograph shows the Rockledge area and the Ibbetson house, which was demolished in 1985. Frank Miller of Riverside's Mission Inn built Villa Rockledge (1918–1929) next door; it is listed in the National Register of Historic Places. Farther south is South Laguna, which was annexed by Laguna Beach in 1988.

77

The 1920s view looks north down South Coast Boulevard, a dirt road prior to 1926, into downtown's center. The old Laguna Beach Hotel, built in 1895, can be seen on the left behind the eucalyptus trees, and at the extreme right is the old Mills Café. Today, most of the buildings on the right side have been replaced with many popular restaurants and shops, and at the bottom of the hill, South Coast Highway veers to the left at the corner of Forest Avenue.

78 — SOUTH LAGUNA BEACH EXPANDS ALONG ITS PICTURESQUE SHORELINE

South Coast Highway in this 1940s image is passing Cleo Street (center) and approaching downtown Laguna. Prior to 1926, this area, known as Nate Brooks's Gulch at Sleepy Hollow, between the separate towns of Laguna Beach and Arch Beach, was impassable for wheeled vehicles. Sleepy Hollow's most famous resident was silent film actor Slim Summerville, whose home is now the Beach House Restaurant. The building seen in the historical photograph at the left corner of Cleo Street is today the Orange Inn at 703 South Coast Highway.

South Laguna Beach Expands Along Its Picturesque Shoreline

William Mortensen began his photographic career taking portraits of Hollywood actors and film stills, and in 1931, he moved to the artist community of Laguna Beach, where he opened his school of photography. He authored several influential books on photographic technique, and his works are held in many of the important museums of photography worldwide. Mortensen died on August 12, 1965, at the age of 68, and today, his former studio, designed by architect Aubrey St. Clair, is the Second Reef Surf Shop at 1020 South Coast Highway.

The Brayton Laguna Pottery building at 1450 South Coast Highway, built in 1928, is part of the art center. Durlin Brayton, a graduate of the Art Institute of Chicago, introduced a line of simple earthenware dishes that were probably the first of their kind in the United States. Brayton's wife, Ellen, helped propel his business to a successful commercial enterprise, and Brayton Laguna Pottery became one of the foremost companies in the history of southern California pottery. Brayton died in 1951, and the shop closed its doors in 1968.

Envisioned by its builder and local artist, City Councilman William W. Riddell, construction of the Hotel La Casa del Camino was completed in 1929. This early 1930s image shows the hotel at the corner of Cress Street and South Coast Highway, situated on a bluff overlooking the Pacific Ocean. It became a retreat for artists, movie stars, and other famous people of the day. Today, the renovated hotel still shows Mediterranean-style old world charm and is a hot spot in the HIP District, particularly the Rooftop at happy hour.

South Laguna Beach Expands Along Its Picturesque Shoreline

This late 1940s photograph shows the Coast Inn at 1401 South Coast Highway, built in 1929 by John "Pappy" Smith. His granddaughter, Carolyn Smith Burris, got the idea for a restaurant and bar attached to the Coast Inn and called it the Seven Seas. Initially frequented by families and the military (who coined the name Boom Boom Room), it eventually became a favorite for the gay community. Today, the turrets are gone, and there are controversial plans to renovate the blufftop building as a boutique hotel with a wine bar.

SOUTH LAGUNA BEACH EXPANDS ALONG ITS PICTURESQUE SHORELINE

The Pottery Shack, shown in the 1940s, was located at the southeast corner of Brooks Street and South Coast Highway. Established in 1936, it was in business for 66 years as a destination for residents and visitors perusing stacks of pottery and collectibles. The founding Leroy B. Childs family retired in 1972 and sold their business; today, the Pottery Shack has been restored as the Old Pottery Place, providing a home for an array of distinctive shops and food for visitors from around the globe.

In 1887, the first pier to be constructed in Laguna Beach was at Arch Beach near the end of Diamond Street. The pier, seen in this 1890s photograph, was built by two homesteading farmers, Nate Brooks and Hubbard Goff, to load barley hay onto a schooner for shipment to San Diego. Guests of the Arch Beach Hotel, which was on a bluff overlooking this area, also used the pier to fish or take an evening stroll. Storms eventually washed the pier away.

South Laguna Beach Expands Along Its Picturesque Shoreline

This 1916 photograph shows the South Coast Highway as a dirt road that followed the contours of the land. It was depicted in a famous oil painting by William Wendt titled *The Old Coast Road*. The home in the clump of trees at left center was originally built in 1907 and was owned by the Ibbetson family. Riverside Mission Inn's Frank Miller built Villa Rockledge next door in 1921. The graded highway has dramatically altered the area. Today's Rockledge Street is at left center.

The house at the end of Arch Street was built in 1918 and was the home and studio of William Wendt and Julia Bracken. He was known as the dean of southern California landscape painters and was a founder of the Laguna Beach Art Association. Julia Bracken Wendt was a successful sculptor who designed medallions. This house was on old Coast Boulevard, but due to grading when South Coast Highway was built in 1926, it is now high above, with Arch Street no longer going through to Coast Highway.

SOUTH LAGUNA BEACH EXPANDS ALONG ITS PICTURESQUE SHORELINE

Hubbard Goff built the Arch Beach Hotel in 1887; Arch Beach was then a separate village, getting a post office two years before Laguna. The hotel closed and in 1895 was moved in sections forming part of the Laguna Beach Hotel. Newspaper publisher Charles Prisk had the Norman-style oceanfront home at 1991 Ocean Way built in 1929; it is shown in the modern photograph at right center, with a large seawall. The actress Bette Davis owned the home in the early 1940s. Woods Cove was once owned by industrialist Harry Edwin Woods after he left Victor, Colorado.

Aliso Beach was a popular location to car camp, as seen in this c. 1920 photograph. The South Coast Highway, at upper right, afforded easy access to the parking lot. The original Aliso Creek and its surroundings were once a formidable barrier to travelers, but pioneer Joseph S. Thurston created the Aliso Canyon Wagon Trail and the Old Coast Wagon Trail, which opened up this area. Today this location is called the Aliso Beach Park, and it has easy access for public parking but no camping.

South Laguna Beach Expands Along Its Picturesque Shoreline

Today, Table Rock Beach is one of the most beautiful beaches found in South Laguna Beach, and public access stairs are found one block north of the Coyote Grill restaurant at 31621 South Coast Highway. In the early days of movie making, Laguna Beach was popular for its picturesque coastline, and this 1925 photograph shows a realistic-looking lighthouse (called the Eagle Rock Lighthouse) that was actually a prop for the movie *Captain January*, released in 1924.

The Victoria Tower, seen in the early 1940s photograph, is a beach access stairway for a French Provincial Revival house above Victoria Beach and is one of Laguna's most noted landmarks. The home (out of view) was constructed in 1926 along with the 60-foot tower by state senator William E. Brown from Los Angeles; in the early 1940s, the home was acquired by Harold Kendrick, a retired naval officer who delighted children by giving them treats for correct answers to his many questions. Actress Bette Midler at one time owned this home.

South Laguna Beach Expands Along Its Picturesque Shoreline

Victoria Beach, seen in this 1940s photograph, is a highly desired neighborhood in Laguna Beach and was once home to notable celebrities, including Bette Midler and Ozzie and Harriet Nelson. Fishing from the rocks was a popular activity when the historic photograph was taken, but in 2012 the State Marine Life Protection Act (with help from various groups including the Laguna Bluebelt Coalition) was implemented in southern California to protect the state's marine life and habitats, and fishing is no longer allowed.

The first homesteader in South Laguna was Eugene Salter in 1870, with later homesteaders taking up farming beans and melons. Unlike downtown Laguna Beach, South Laguna did not become commercialized and remained an unincorporated part of Orange County until being annexed into the City of Laguna Beach in 1988. The village area of the South Laguna is shown in this early 1950s photograph, and little change is visible when compared to the modern image.

SOUTH LAGUNA BEACH EXPANDS ALONG ITS PICTURESQUE SHORELINE

In 1960, South Laguna was unincorporated, and Martha Ray Real Estate was in business at the corner of Third Avenue and South Coast Highway. At the time, a two-bedroom home with a view could be had for $37,500! Television antennas were tenuously wired on roofs. The City of Laguna Beach annexed South Laguna in 1988, and this corner is now the Performance Racing Industry offices at 31706 South Coast Highway. The development high on the ridge line is out of the city's control, being in the city of Laguna Niguel.

94   South Laguna Beach Expands Along Its Picturesque Shoreline

Spread along an ocean bluff in South Laguna Beach was the Treasure Island Mobile Home Park. Built in the 1940s, it offered a panoramic view of the Pacific Ocean for residents. However, increasing property value and higher rents combined to close the park, and in 1998, approval was given to build a luxury resort. In 2003, a resort and hotel known as the Montage opened. Additionally, the public Treasure Island Park was constructed with access to the beach. It is maintained by the hotel.

SOUTH LAGUNA BEACH EXPANDS ALONG ITS PICTURESQUE SHORELINE

DISCOVER THOUSANDS OF LOCAL HISTORY BOOKS FEATURING MILLIONS OF VINTAGE IMAGES

Arcadia Publishing, the leading local history publisher in the United States, is committed to making history accessible and meaningful through publishing books that celebrate and preserve the heritage of America's people and places.

Find more books like this at
www.arcadiapublishing.com

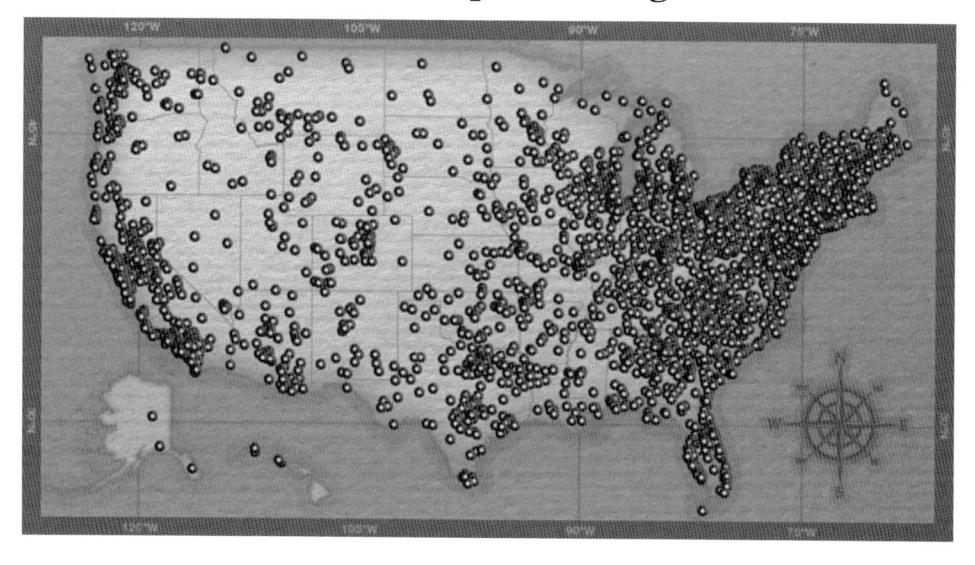

Search for your hometown history, your old stomping grounds, and even your favorite sports team.

Consistent with our mission to preserve history on a local level, this book was printed in South Carolina on American-made paper and manufactured entirely in the United States. Products carrying the accredited Forest Stewardship Council (FSC) label are printed on 100 percent FSC-certified paper.

MADE IN THE USA